High School Students Earning College Credit

High School Students Earning College Credit

A Guide to Creating Dual–Credit Programs

Margaret Fincher-Ford

CORWIN PRESS, INC.
A Sage Publications Company
Thousand Oaks, California

For information address:

Corwin Press, Inc.
A Sage Publications Company
2455 Teller Road
Thousand Oaks, California 91320
e-mail: order@corwin.sagepub.com

SAGE Publications Ltd.
6 Bonhill Street
London EC2A 4PU
United Kingdom

SAGE Publications India Pvt. Ltd.
M-32 Market
Greater Kailash I
New Delhi 110 048 India

Printed in the United States of America

Library of Congress Cataloging-in-Publication Data

Fincher-Ford, Margaret.
    High school students earning college credit : a guide to creating
dual-credit programs / author, Margaret Fincher-Ford.
        p.   cm.
    ISBN 0-8039-6549-4 (cloth : acid-free paper). — ISBN
0-8039-6550-8 (pbk. : acid-free paper)
    1. Advanced placement programs (Education). 2. College credits—
United States. 3. School credits—United States. 4. High school
students—United States.   I. Title.
LB2359.5.F55   1997
378.1′65—dc20   96-35701

This book is printed on acid-free paper.

97 98 99 00 01 10 9 8 7 6 5 4 3 2 1

Corwin Press Production Editor: S. Marlene Head
Editorial Assistant: Nicole Fountain
Typesetter: Rebecca Evans
Cover Designer: Marcia R. Finlayson

Contents

[FINCHER-FORD page viii — half-title]

Preface

The process that is described in this book, dual credit, which allows high school students to earn both high school and college credit, came to fruition in a very predictable, almost deterministic way. In 1991, as Dean of Instructional Services at a suburban community college, I was contacted by the area high school principal and was asked if I would design a dual-credit program. I knew vaguely about dual credit but had not seen references in the educational literature. The principal had not seen references either. His primary concern was how quickly we could research and implement the program to respond to a parent's request. The parent making the request had recently relocated to the new school district from another region where the community college and the high school had developed a dual-credit program. Consequently, the principal said, "The parent is ecstatic that her daughter was able to accumulate 18 semester college credit hours prior to high school graduation. At the other end of the spectrum, the parent is disappointed that a similar agreement is not available in this locale. She has a son who is a 'college prep' sophomore, and she wants him to accumulate as many college credit hours as possible while still in high school."

After talking to the principal and identifying the parameters, timetable, and specific needs, I began an extensive investigation on dual credit in state, national, and international venues. In the process of gathering information, it was apparent that a few school districts and community colleges were participating in quite successful arrangements, but there were absolutely no written rules, guidelines, recommendations for implementation, or caveats. Thus, during the next 12 months, while developing the dual-credit plan, I interviewed, by telephone and in person, over 150 high school administrators and teachers, college academicians, accrediting agency personnel, school board representatives, legislators, coordinating board representatives, and parents before finally formalizing the first dual-credit agreement for the school district in September 1992.

Since 1992, the dual-credit program within that school district has flourished. That program has expanded into neighboring school districts, counties, and regions. As the number of dual-credit programs is steadily increasing, and so are the enrollments, there is still very little "how-to" information in print that will allow for replication in other communities. This book provides just such helpful how-to information based upon empirical data derived from high school and community college administrators from across the nation.

Hopefully, this book will be useful to practitioners (administrators and teachers) in developing dual-credit educational partnerships. It will also be beneficial to students by providing information and access to a broader continuum of learning. The continuum will, in effect, increase opportunities for capable students to progress through their programs of study at an accelerated pace. Additionally, this work can serve as a companion text to other major resources in the professional preparation of teachers and administrators at educational institutions throughout the nation. Conceivably, students enrolled in an array of education courses (Curriculum and Instruction, Foundations of Education, Philosophy of Education, and Educational Leadership) could benefit from (a) an analysis of the dual-credit process and (b) the application of the dual-credit process to their specific field of education. Alternatively, this work could be used in workshop settings by practicing professionals who desire continuing education credit or inservice training in curriculum development with a specific focus on the design of dual-credit programs for their school districts.

The contents of this work focus on an educational process that creates a network of success for all stakeholder groups in the community: students, parents, the educational enterprise, the community at large, and the greater society in general. Chapter 1 provides the historical foundation and the global context for a dual-credit educational model. A call to action is mounted based on data that show the high dropout rate of students, the escalating costs of education, and the unnecessary duplication of courses in high school and in postsecondary education.

Chapter 2 addresses the intricacies of planning a dual-credit program for public and private institutions. The reader is alerted to specific issues that must be addressed and to effective "resolution" strategies. Because many students are interested in pursuing a college degree or certificate, Chapter 3 provides a "Rosetta stone" approach to identifying courses that fulfill both high school and college credit. This approach should result in cost savings for students while simultaneously providing a college education that fully prepares students for success in college or for transfer to a senior-level institution. Chapter 4 details how to establish program effectiveness via an array of accountability measures. Assessment instruments are included for potential use.

Chapter 5 provides an annotated sample of a dual-credit agreement with clarifying comments about components of the process. The sample could conceivably be used as a "boilerplate" formula for dual-credit initiatives that will be developed in school districts.

Chapter 6 clarifies the differences between dual credit and articulated credit and presents a plan to use when high school and college teams meet to articulate courses that will be credited toward a high school diploma and a college degree. Chapter 7 is a critically important one. It establishes the vital importance of faculty and the deterministic roles they play in the success or failure of the dual-credit plan. Because faculty members must design, develop, and implement the program, reason dictates that they should also be involved in programmatic planning. Thus, Chapter 7 provides a faculty inclusion methodology for systemic change.

Each chapter provides a reference glossary of terms to acquaint the reader with the terms' usage. Finally, the book concludes with discussion questions that are provided to generate thoughtful discussions, prepare the reader for group-oriented forums on dual-credit programs, and accelerate an educational philosophy that promotes an expanded continuum of learning.

Margaret Fincher-Ford
Houston, Texas
October 1996

About the Author

Margaret Fincher-Ford is Vice Chancellor for Instructional Services at the Houston Community College System. Previously, she taught English at the university and community college levels before becoming a community college administrator. She completed her doctorate in Curriculum and Instruction at the University of Houston in 1979.

In 1991, when Fincher-Ford was Dean of Instructional Services, she researched, developed, and implemented a dual-credit program within the community college district. That program is now flourishing with student enrollments. One of her recent articles, titled "Dual Credit Should Be Institutionalized," appears in the journal *Alliance*, a publication of the National Center for Urban Partnerships. Fincher-Ford has published articles and resource textbooks in higher education and has conducted workshops, seminars, and symposia at national and international meetings. Some of the topics on which she has presented include Dual Credit, Teaching Effectiveness, Educational Leadership, and Preparing America's Workforce for the 21st Century.

Objectives of Dual-Credit Programs

As you read this book, keep in mind that the primary objectives of dual-credit programs are to

- Create a continuum of learning from high school to college
- Shorten the time required for high school students to complete an undergraduate degree
- Eliminate the duplication of courses taken in high school and in college
- Sharpen students' general academic preparedness for college
- Expand the academic options for college-bound students
- Enhance the college-credit options for technical education (or tech prep) students

1

Earning High School and College Credit

Introduction

In many parts of the United States, high school students are enrolling in college-level courses for both high school and college credit. This educational innovation is referred to as *dual credit*, a process that is predicated upon formalized agreements between high schools, community colleges, and some universities. The far-reaching implications of dual credit are phenomenal and are heralded by school districts and community colleges alike as an educational innovation that will "blaze a trail" for successful educational partnerships into the 21st century. The most notable effect of dual-credit programs is the accelerated time at which high school students can matriculate through their educational programs of study.

Interviews conducted with high school and college administrators reflect their positive attitudes about dual-credit programs. They characterize dual credit as an educational option that creates a continuum of education for high school students who will pursue a postsecondary degree or certificate after high school graduation.

Few works have been published that explain the process one would use to create a dual-credit program, the problems that will be encountered, the positive and negative experiences, and ultimately, recommendations and caveats. This information vacuum exists despite the fact that some schools have quietly experimented with dual credit for a number of years.

At this time, however, the proliferation of dual-credit programs throughout the nation requires definitive guidelines by state coordinating boards, accrediting agencies, and experienced practitioners to ensure high standards and a quality education for students.

The dual-credit implementation model described in this book has engendered surprising enthusiasm among high school students, their parents, and postsecondary (primarily community college) administrators. Principally, dual credit breaks a proverbial glass ceiling that heretofore governed students' passage through high school; simultaneously, it provides students with early admission into a more advanced level of learning for which they, upon successful completion of the course, immediately receive college credit. In the traditional system of high school education, the advanced level of learning and earning college credit were held in abeyance until some future date. With dual credit, the future is now.

High school students are now challenged to look beyond their current status and to dual-enroll in courses that will apply toward their college degree or skilled profession. Parent and teacher association groups are ecstatic to learn about the vast educational opportunities now available to students; high schools and community colleges are pleased about the furtherance of their mission to "build communities" and to facilitate student success. The schools and their administrative teams are pleased about the collateral benefits, for dual-credit partnerships help to build a broad base of community support—socially, economically, and politically.

The Problem

National statistics show the high student dropout rate among high school students. Data show that many students, primarily ethnic minorities, enroll in school but often leave without the diploma, skills, or expertise to earn a salary above the minimum wage. Of course, some factors leading to dropout cannot be controlled by the schools: family problems, relocation, loss of employment. But those factors that can be controlled should be identified by school district personnel, and intervention strategies should be developed to chart a course for each student's success. The preponderance of literature shows that one specific problem that high school students have involves what is viewed as a discrete curriculum that appears unrelated to their daily lives.

Additionally, educational literature shows that many schools, secondary and postsecondary, still require uniform "seat-time" hours for students to matriculate through a program of study, irrespective of the students' levels of academic preparedness or readiness. The problem is further exacerbated by the duplication of secondary and postsecondary courses, the attendant escalating costs these duplications incur, and the lack of discernible benefits derived from such duplications.

Trend analysis studies are replete with examples that confirm the consequences of educating students in "the same old way" as in the past. Almost exclusively, the high dropout rate is the end result. So the question is, How can leaders help create the educational nexus for students to stir their desire to stay in school, excel, and break the stereotypical mold that, based upon demographics, perpetuates a myth? The high school to college dual-credit programs have helped to shift the tide. Interviews with high school and college administrators, teachers, and students confirm the successes of those students who had the opportunity to earn college credit while still in high school. Over the last several years, testimonials have been shared by parents who attribute the high performance of their children to aggressive educational programs that challenge students and that are relevant—both to their present and to their future.

Historical Context for Dual Credit

For well over a century, educational leaders have recognized the need for high schools and postsecondary institutions to partner together in meaningful ways—ways that enhance teaching and learning. In the 1880s, the Massachusetts Teachers' Association passed two resolutions that led to partnerships between high schools and postsecondary institutions. One of the resolutions stated that the lack of cooperation between high schools and colleges was an evil. The second resolution stated that more cooperation between the schools and higher education would be a positive good. Thus, between 1892 and 1918, the National Education Association convened a series of meetings to formulate a plan for cooperation between the public schools and institutions of higher education.

In 1892, the president of Harvard University, Charles Eliot, chaired a committee on Secondary School Studies to evaluate the conditions of the secondary school curriculum. Foremost in his study was the claim that the high school curriculum represented a disordered array of courses. This committee, referred to as the "Committee of Ten," represented the first attempt, nationally, to standardize the high school curriculum and to coordinate secondary and postsecondary education. The outcome of the committee's work acknowledged the terminal and college preparatory functions of the high school. However, the committee recommended curriculum entirely oriented toward the college-bound student. In effect, the Committee of Ten established priority for college preparation as a primary function of the high school curriculum. Thus the terminal students would be given the same program of study as those headed for college.

Although substantial groundwork had been laid for secondary and postsecondary cooperation, the progressive movement on partnership programs did not materialize until the Sputnik crisis in the fall of 1957. The launching of Sputnik I created open criticism of the American education system. The Soviet Union's success in launching the first man-made satellite into orbit ignited smoldering criticisms of influential individuals and interest groups who had repeatedly accused the public high schools of weakening academic standards. Thus the Sputnik crisis resulted in governmental programs that sought the integration of secondary and postsecondary studies.

Integration of programs began immediately, but the first configuration of a secondary and postsecondary dual-credit partnership did not occur until years later with Syracuse University's Project Advance in the early 1970s (Gaines & Wilbur, 1985; Wilbur & Chapman, 1978). Other institutions throughout the country began to implement similar programs. With the release of the report *A Nation At Risk* (Gardner et al., 1983), incendiary statements spread throughout the nation regarding the efficacy of secondary education. In response, many states implemented a plan to raise the performance of all students and to simultaneously increase the number of academic courses required for high school graduation. Dual credit was one of the programmatic options that was implemented in some school districts throughout the country.

A review of the literature and interviews with school district and community college leaders throughout the nation show that dual-credit programs have operated since the early 1970s in some sectors of the country. Nevertheless, the number of dual-credit partnerships did not begin to increase significantly until the 1980s. For example, St. Petersburg Junior College and the Pinellas County School System realized that the dual-credit program could be a means of challenging the best high school students through accelerated learning. Their program has been sharpened over the years and is a success even today; they attribute that success to executive commitment that has been communicated to all members of the team.

The College Now Program at Johnson County Community College (JCCC) in Overland Park, Kansas, was initiated in the fall of 1984. The JCCC program is nationally recognized for its success in helping students make the transition from high school to college.

In 1982, the State of Texas approved dual credit between high schools and community colleges, and in 1994 a more advanced initiative, called the Advanced High School Program, was introduced. Community colleges in various parts of Texas began implementing dual-credit programs with great success: Midland Community College, Dallas County Community College System, Del Mar College, and Houston Community College System are among some of the many Texas institutions to implement variations of the dual-credit program and have track records of student success. The Virginia Community College District entered into an agreement with the Virginia Department of Education to offer dual-credit courses to Virginia high school students in September 1988.

Executive commitment to the program has resulted in educational partnerships that are of high quality and that meet the needs of students. The list of dual-credit partnerships continues ad infinitum, and the list of positive reports about the successes of the programs and of students are just as lengthy.

Dual-credit programs should be institutionalized. Many school districts have not implemented them, however, because of (a) a lack of information on how to get started and (b) uninformed skepticism among academic purists who believe that their canon will be compromised.

Dual-credit programs consistently create opportunities and real incentives for high school students to work hard academically, explore their educational interests before full-time college study, review various career options, and understand what is required of them to be successful in a career or profession.

The primary objectives of dual-credit programs, then and now, remain constant. Those objectives are to smooth the transition from high school to college, shorten the time needed to earn an undergraduate degree, and avoid unnecessary duplication of curricula. The increasing number of partnerships between high schools and postsecondary institutions leads to the conclusion that the second resolution of the Massachusetts Teachers' Association in 1880, which addressed cooperation between high schools and colleges, has resulted in a positive good.

The Dual-Credit Process

The high school and community college partnership has been and continues to be incredibly fertile for many kinds of progressive educational initiatives—dual credit is only one of them. Tech prep is another. Several years ago, for example, information about the Tech Prep Associate in Applied Science (A.A.S.) degree was relatively new. Today, through the efforts of Hull and Parnell (1991), the tech prep movement is a well-received, viable option to college prep. Educators now recognize that the dual-credit option enhances the educational pathways for both tech prep and college prep students.

Currently, there is a national emergence and recognition of dual-credit programs. As a result of this emergence, many regional accrediting agencies acknowledge dual-credit programmatic partnerships; these agencies define standards and criteria for an assessment of programmatic quality and effectiveness. Thus, during an institution's initial accreditation visit, dual-credit classes will, as a matter of course, become an integral part of the program evaluation process. Colleges are encouraged to maintain accurate and detailed information regarding courses offered; course curricula (syllabi and outlines); faculty credentials, including official transcripts; student enrollments; and student outcomes.

In some states, the dual-credit process agreement between high schools and colleges allows students to enroll as early as the 10th and 11th grades. Twelfth-grade enrollments, however, are the norm. If students are allowed to take the maximum course load during their senior year, they can conceivably have enough college credit hours accumulated by the time they graduate to be classified as a second-semester freshman. It cannot be overemphasized that dual-credit courses are college courses that fulfill both college and high school objectives and competencies. The college requirements and standards, however, should be more academically rigorous and challenging than the standards and requirements of the high school course.

Reference Glossary

Continuum of education. A barrier-free, seamless approach to education that allows students access to differing levels of study based upon student academic preparedness and readiness.

Dual credit. A process by which a student enrolls in a course at one institution for credit and, upon enrollment at a second institution of a different level, also receives credit for the same course at the second institution.

Dual enrollment. A process by which a student is enrolled simultaneously, usually at different educational levels, for training or courses of study.

2

Getting Started
With the Planning Phase

Because each school district is different, there is not a given, pre-ferred formula for getting started with the planning phase for dual-credit programs. It is important, however, that administrative personnel from either the high school or the college initiate the planning discussions. Several examples illustrate the diverse beginnings of the planning phase with three distinct school districts.

In one very affluent school district, after the dual-credit model had been completed, the principal invited the college administration to speak to a parents' advisory group about dual credit. The parents were impressed with the dual-credit proposal and asked the principal to pursue piloting the dual-credit program during the next academic year. In this instance, the parents' advisory group was the catalyst behind the planning and implementation process.

In another school district, the college administrator provided the school district personnel with a proposal for a dual-credit partnership. Several weeks later, the school district administrators invited the college instructional administrators to a meeting to discuss the planning process. In this instance, the process was driven by the college.

A third school district hosted a morning meeting at an outdoor learning center to explore how dual credit might complement its existing tech prep program. Academic and technical administrators, as well as department heads from the high school and nearby college, were present. In this instance, the planning process was driven by the high school's technical area.

Whatever the driving force behind the dual-credit process, it is important that the dual-credit program be carefully conceived, carefully designed, and frequently evaluated and that all guidelines that impact accreditation and the integrity of the college curricula and course transferability be maintained.

High School and College Discipline Teams

In planning the dual-credit process, the astute administrator will insist that discipline teams be formed. Discipline teams will allow high school and college faculty who teach similar courses to meet, learn about the others' disciplines, evaluate curricula, and make dual-credit course recommendations. Without doubt, faculty involvement is absolutely essential at this stage to maintain the integrity of the instructional process and to leave curricula evaluation decisions within the control and purview of faculty where such decisions naturally reside.

Discipline teams are very important to the credibility of the dual-credit process. Furthermore, the teams are important for reasons that relate directly to pedagogical soundness:

- Both groups understand their curricula and can address what is required to fulfill the competencies and objectives for the semester.
- The combined high school and college discipline teams are the preferred group to recommend to their peers and to their respective administrative groups whether dual-credit offerings in their respective subject areas should be approved, not approved, continued, or discontinued.
- The discipline teams are able to monitor whether the integrity of the curriculum is being maintained and whether standards are being upheld.

An example of a Dual-Credit Competency Analysis is shown in Table 2.1. The competency analysis provides a format that discipline

TABLE 2.1 Dual-Credit Course Objectives and Competency Analysis

A Worksheet

College name: _____   Name of independent school
                                     district: _____

College number: _____   Course title: _____

Course contact hours: _____   Course number: _____

Course textbook: _____   Contact hours: _____

                                     Course textbook: _____

College objectives and competencies taught[a]	Check matches	Independent school district objectives and competencies taught[a]
1.		1.
2.		2.
3.		3.
4.		4.

Discipline contact   *Discipline contact*

Person: _____   Person: _____

Telephone number: _____   Telephone number: _____

Date: _____   Date: _____

Comments:

---

a. This page represents one model to use. Please use additional pages to add competencies.

teams can use to compare the high school course ("essential elements") competencies and objectives with those of the college. Whenever the discipline teams agree that the objectives and/or competencies of the courses coincide, dual credit will likely be recommended. Conversely, when the objectives and competencies do not match, discipline teams will likely indicate that dual credit is not recommended. The discipline teams should use the worksheet during their meetings to reach consensus on which courses will or will not be recommended and the rationale for their decision making.

Because school boards are responsible for acting as final authority on institutional matters, both the high school and the college boards of trustees should review and approve the general dual-credit agreement shown in Table 2.2 (see also Chapter 5). The chief executive officers (CEOs) of the institutions—the superintendent and the college president or chancellor—should then sign the course plan that follows or a tailor-made variation of the course plan. If they sign the plan at the board meeting on the same day that the dual-credit agreement is approved (see Chapter 5), then it is recommended that all signatures, save for those of the CEOs, appear on the course plan in advance. To make the signing official and to ceremoniously promote the cause in the media, the CEOs would then sign the Dual-Credit Course Plan at the board meeting.

Issues for Team Review

During the planning phase, discipline team members will need clear directions, clarification of terminology, and, most of all, reassurance that the new initiative does not threaten job security. Administrators should be sensitive to these concerns and seek to address them in a forthright manner.

In the clarification process, one of the team's first goals, for instance, might be to distinguish a competency from an objective. Whether the administrator knows it or not, the evaluation process begins at this point. Faculty members begin to assess just how knowledgeable and confident the leader is about the process. So administrators should be equipped with explanations and meaningful examples, and keep in mind that objectives and competencies are quite similar. Objectives state in "active" terms what a student will know or be able to do upon completing an activity. Competencies state in "measurable" performance terms what a person who completes an activity will know and be able to do, and the accompanying level of mastery required.

TABLE 2.2 Dual-Credit Course Agreement Plan

This document is an attachment to the official Dual-Credit Agreement (see Chapter 5) that was approved for implementation by the board of trustees on _____.

College name: _____   Name of independent school
                                    district: _____

College number: _____   Course title: _____

Course contact hours: _____   Course number: _____

Course textbook: _____   Contact hours: _____

                                    Course textbook: _____

College objectives and competencies taught[a]	Check matches	Independent school district objectives and competencies taught[a]
1.		1.
2.		2.
Please check one of the boxes.	Comments	
☐ Dual Credit is recommended.		
☐ Dual Credit is not recommended.		

Signatures

College   *School District*

_____   _____
Department Chair   Signature/Title

_____   _____
Dean   Signature/Title

_____   _____
Vice President, Instruction   Signature/Title

_____   _____
President   Superintendent

a. This page represents one model to use. Please use additional pages to add competencies.

Other issues for team review relate to the different state, federal, and accrediting agency requirements for colleges and high schools. For example, in one state that was surveyed, the coordinating board for higher education stipulates that technical instructors who teach college courses must have 3 years of work experience in business or industry. The state agency that oversees public schools, on the other hand, stipulates that 2 years of work experience are required. If courses are offered for dual high school and college credit, then the standards for postsecondary education must be followed when hiring faculty.

A prominent fear among some faculty who are told about the dual-credit process concerns job security. Empirical research data show that this fear is unwarranted. First and foremost, criteria are used in the hiring of faculty. College faculty must meet specific accrediting agency criteria and state guidelines before being employed to teach college-level courses. Similarly, high school teachers must also be certified according to specific local, state, and accreditation agency criteria before they are eligible to teach high school courses. In nationwide interviews, no evidence surfaced that faculty members at either the high school or college level have lost their jobs because of dual-credit arrangements. Nor has any evidence surfaced that indicates their jobs are in any way jeopardized. Quite the contrary, faculty have become greater assets to the school district and to the community. Interviews indicate that opportunities have opened for high school faculty to pursue further graduate study. No reports have indicated that college faculty, however, have left their assignments to pursue high school teaching. In the end analysis, reports from school administrators show that fears subside when faculty have an opportunity to meet, interact, and develop a working rapport and professional respect for one another.

Addressing Faculty Members' Concerns

Early on in the partnering process, efforts should be made, nonetheless, to address faculty members' concerns. The following is a multistage (personal, collegial, administrative) approach to addressing faculty members' issues, both real and imagined, regarding the dual-credit partnership. If the issues are resolved during the first stage, then the remaining stages can be ignored. If issues still remain, the succeeding stages should be explored.

Stage 1: Personal

Stage 1 allows teachers to address their concerns privately through self-reflection. If teachers are feeling uncertain about the initiative, they should try to answer candidly the following clarifying questions:

- Based upon what I know, what is the purpose of a dual-credit partnership?
- Why do I feel anxious about a partnership that will benefit my students?
- Based upon what I know, what resources can I contribute to support the partnership?
- What can I do, short of abandoning the process, to alleviate my anxiety?
- If I participate in this process, how can I best exercise control over what happens in my discipline?
- Am I uneasy about this process because of territoriality, fear of job security, or fear of change?
- If my fear relates to job security, is there something I have done to create this dynamic?
- Is the college teacher certified according to state guidelines, accrediting agency guidelines, and teacher training course work to teach high school courses?
- Is the college teacher really interested in teaching high school courses, or do I have other insecurities that are surfacing?
- If my job is not in fact threatened, and if I can control what happens in my discipline, then why would I continue to resist change?
- How will this new initiative create opportunities for me?
- How will the new initiative benefit my students?
- How will the new initiative benefit the school and my community?

Stage 2: Collegial

If there are still unresolved issues from Stage 1 that impede the working relationship among discipline teams, then the Stage 2 questions should be discussed during the meetings of the small group discipline teams.

- How are you feeling about this type of partnership between our schools?
- How will this partnership benefit the students, the school, and the community?
- What can we do, short of abandoning the process, to address our fears or anxieties? Do we need to include specific recommendations in the agreement that the board will approve, or should the course plan include strict requirements in the comments section that the CEOs will sign?
- Should we stipulate in the agreement that all dual-credit courses offered at the high school should only be taught by certified high school faculty who are also qualified according to the college's criteria?
- What stipulations should be included in the agreement that will create greater comfort for the participants?

Stage 3: Administrative

If, after the discipline teams' discussions, there is still some uncertainty, the school administration should be available to answer questions, from the individuals or from the group, to reassure the faculty members that their active participation in the process will in no way render teaching positions less secure. Administrators should address the following:

- The purpose for participating in the dual-credit process
- How the process will benefit the students, the school, and the community
- The fact that teachers' jobs are secure and are not threatened by the partnership
- The willingness to incorporate specific provisos in the agreement that will protect the rights of high school and college faculty and the integrity of the curriculum
- Reassurances that programmatic standards will be maintained

Instruction of Dual-Credit Courses

Regional accrediting agencies have specific requirements for faculty members who are hired to teach college courses. The college administration should, therefore, refer to the accrediting agency criteria for their specific region and uphold all standards and criteria. Interviews confirm that limited numbers of high school teachers have credentials in specific subject areas, as required by the regional accrediting agencies, to teach college-transferable courses; therefore, the dual-credit course offerings should be limited to those specific courses that the school district faculty are qualified to teach.

To promote high school–college partnerships in the endeavor, the community college could extend an invitation to the local university to seek approval from the state's authorizing agency to provide graduate-level instruction at remote sites (perhaps sites owned or leased by the community college) or via distance education to help high school faculty upgrade their credentials. This would be of benefit to the larger community and would eventually increase the pool of qualified faculty who are eligible to teach college-level courses.

In any event, instruction of all dual-credit courses must conform to the standards of the college. Although interviews with school district personnel revealed a number of diverse arrangements, the least favorable would be to assign an inexperienced college teacher to the high school campus. This arrangement is undesirable because it can function as a gateway to a variety of controversies and potentially problematic situations for both the high school and the college. The issue of academic freedom and other, even more divisive issues might arise that the partnership could easily avoid.

The Planning Process and Integration
of Dual Credit and Tech Prep

Dual credit can be used to enhance students' educational opportunities regardless of whether their area of focus is academic or technical. Several questions that will guide the planning discussion follow; these should be addressed during the teams' early meetings.

- Would you like to offer dual credit in both the academic and technical program areas at your institution?

- Where will the dual-credit courses be taught—at the high school location, at a centralized location, or at the college site?
- At what hours of the day will the course(s) be offered?
- What courses are you considering for dual credit?
- Does the high school have qualified faculty to teach the courses?
- Does the high school wish to have the dual-credit courses taught at the zero hour of the school day?
- Does the school district want to provide one central facility where the college can offer the dual-credit courses to all students in the district at specified times during the day?
- Will there be separate and distinct classes for dual credit or will a "class-within-a-class" approach be used?
- Will dual-credit courses be offered via distance education?

The typical high school semester comprises 90 contact hours, 5 days per week. On the other hand, the typical college semester comprises 48 contact hours per 3-credit-hour course. In some states, the college course can be scheduled in a flexible-entry format; thus the beginning and ending dates would vary. This flexible scheduling format facilitates the community colleges' and high schools' abilities to partner on dual credit much more effectively, thereby providing flexible enrollment dates for more high school students who qualify and want to enroll.

Dual Credit: Enhancing Tech Prep

Dual credit enhances the tech prep process. Dual credit provides an option to articulation and allows students to take dual-credit high school technical courses that are recorded immediately as college credit. This process, in effect, buttresses the efforts of Tech Prep Consortia which, as mandated by the Tech Prep Education Act, implement the following essential elements of tech prep: formal signed articulation agreements; a core of required courses in general academics; inservice training for teachers; training for counselors; equal access for special populations students to all tech prep programs; and preparatory services to help all populations participate in tech prep. In other words, the process used in dual credit can help accomplish the cited objectives of the Tech Prep Education Act.

The process for identifying the technical courses that should be offered for dual credit is similar to the process used for academic courses (see Tables 2.1 and 2.2). The differences might relate to the following, which should be noted in the "Comments" section of the worksheet and used in guiding the team members' discussions and recommendations.

- What are the special licensing or accrediting agency requirements that stipulate the faculty credentials for the technical program?
- What are the site-specific licensing restrictions for offering the course—what constitutes an unlicensed site?
- What are the specific competencies that technical students should acquire that are currently a part of the academic curriculum?

It is certain that dual credit provides a great opportunity for students who are seeking 2-year college transfer degrees (e.g., the associate in arts or associate in science degree), the technical degree that equips students for employment (i.e., the associate in applied science degree), or a college certificate. Because a general academic core of 15 semester–credit hours is required of all degree-seeking students, virtually all students, if they are qualified to enroll in college courses, would benefit from dual credit. Courses in humanities and fine arts, social and behavioral sciences, and natural sciences and mathematics can be taken and transferred to practically any senior-level institution in the country. These courses are also applicable toward the completion of most degrees. However, it is important, as a precautionary measure, that students seek academic counseling and develop an educational degree plan before they take more than 12 academic semester–credit hours. Because many institutions periodically change their program degree requirements, the educational degree plan will serve as a commitment to the student that all courses listed on the degree plan will be honored toward a specific degree at that college or university.

Dual credit and articulated course credit are programmatic complements. Dual credit results in a college transcript and allows students to transfer their credit to a 4-year institution. Articulated credit is awarded once the student completes high school and enrolls at the postsecondary institution that holds the joint articulation agreement.

Expanding the Dual-Credit Net

Interviews with school district administrators reveal that ethnic minority students seldom enroll in dual-credit programs. The rationale these administrators offer is that the students often do not qualify for such rigorous programs of study. Some college personnel dismiss the prospect of offering dual credit in predominantly minority school districts because, they say, "so few students would be enrolled in the classes." Others say they only offer dual credit to the upper 15% of their student population. In an interview with a school administrator in a large urban school district, the administrator said that dual credit is concentrated at select, mostly upper middle-class schools within the district. The dual-credit programs are largely nonexistent in poorer school districts. The obvious question then is, Do minority students know about the program? If so, what do they know? Qualified students, no matter their designation (academic, technical, minority, female, high risk, etc.) should be given the incentive and the opportunity to participate in dual-credit programs, for this may be the very golden opportunity that could transform their lives. The programs' limited availability and the misperceptions of the administrators simply perpetuate a self-fulfilling prophecy that insists minorities could not excel in dual-credit programs.

A high school principal is the visionary for his or her specific school and is, to a large degree, responsible for the successes of the student populations served. Thus each high school principal should review the districtwide approval for dual credit and organize a team to implement the program within the school. This program could provide just the incentive that could result in greater interest in school, a lower dropout rate, and a marked increase in the number of those who choose to pursue a college degree or technical trade after high school graduation.

Quality Control Standards

High schools and colleges should implement measures to monitor the quality of dual-credit courses. Close monitoring and evaluation of the program is essential because of the newness of the dual-credit process. For example, if the course is being taught by the high school teacher, on the high school site, how can the college ensure that the college curriculum is being followed? How will the instructional process be monitored? The close monitoring of the program is not to challenge the integrity or the effectiveness of the teacher; instead, it is intended to maintain program accountability. Quality control is vital and pertains to teachers, course materials, and the effectiveness of classroom instruction. Teachers must meet the criteria for employment as specified by the respective regional accrediting agency. Failure to maintain minimal standards as per the guidelines of accrediting agencies could jeopardize the institution's accreditation status, the institution's standing in the community, and the transferability of courses to senior-level institutions.

In addition to the criterion for qualified faculty, it must also be reiterated that the dual-credit course is a college course. Therefore, all components of the course should reflect the same college-based standards: the same curricula, syllabi, and textbooks. At all costs, avoid lowering standards. For accountability purposes, both intra- and interinstitutionally, the dual-credit instructional program should be evaluated on a regular basis, and both institutions (high school and college) should collect data that provide student success information and total programmatic effectiveness. If there are weaknesses that surface, those weaknesses should be addressed proactively. Reports containing programmatic effectiveness results should be provided to all stakeholder groups, both inside and outside the institutions.

Board Approval

In some states, there are two specific levels of approvals before dual credit can be implemented. The first approval is from the state, and the second is from the local school and community college districts. Be sure that approvals are in place at all levels before offering dual-credit classes (see Table 2.3). If the approvals are not in place, the students, technically, cannot be awarded the dual credit, and the college cannot receive contact-hour funding.

Once the dual-credit agreements are completed, the board chairs of both institutions (high school and college) should sign the agreement, preferably at a board meeting. This process formalizes the partnership that was created to serve the student population and the

TABLE 2.3 Dual-Credit Checklist of Approvals

Do you have state approval?	Yes	No
Legislature		
State secondary education agency		
Higher education agency		

Do you have local approval?	Yes	No
School district board		
Community college board		

community. In all instances, the partnering institutions should seek press coverage whenever there are such educational agreements. This type of exposure informs the community that two public institutions are addressing its educational needs in a deliberate and responsible manner.

Financial and Logistical Issues

When dual credit is being considered, check with the coordinating board of the state to determine whether the practice of dual credit will or will not constitute financial "double-dipping." If there is no coordinating board in the state, then there should be a higher education council or a council of college presidents or school administrators. In addition to checking the authorizing agency, the schools' administration should contact the state's education agency for public secondary education to determine what implications exist for implementing the dual-credit plan. The finance division of either entity (Coordinating Board for Higher Education or State Education Agency for Public Schools) can quickly provide information on funding matters for high schools and community colleges.

If the state does not have legislation that permits dual-credit partnerships between high schools and community colleges, this is an opportune time for stakeholder groups to talk to their secondary and postsecondary advocates, including boards of trustees and legislators, about introducing legislation for dual credit, which will be a long-term benefit for the state. The next section offers sample language that specifies the conditions under which high school credit is to be awarded for college courses.

When the faculty member is a full-time employee of the school district, the dual-credit agreement should specify the stipend amount that the college will pay the faculty member to teach the course. All methods of payment should abide by all standards of compliance for the state. Interviews disclosed different configurations of remunerating the high school instructors who teach dual-credit courses. Some high school teachers are paid the standard stipend received by the college's part-time faculty. In other situations, the college and the high school both contribute to the stipend. And in other instances, high school teachers' pay was calculated based upon the number of students enrolled in the course. Before finalizing any agreement, the school administration should ask the state to provide information about preferred pay plans and whether there are hidden issues that should be addressed in the agreement.

So, as a rule of thumb, institutions that start dual-credit programs should request guidance from the state coordinating board. The state legislation should be reviewed, and the high school and college oversight agencies should be contacted regarding (a) their rules for claiming student attendance and (b) their recommendations for paying full-time high school teachers who instruct dual-credit courses.

In Texas, the Commissioners of Education (K–12 and postsecondary) developed a proposal to identify and eliminate duplication of state funding in response to a legislative house bill (House Bill No. 1336) that addresses courses for joint high school and junior college credit. In the proposal, the commissioners identified the number of hours students must be in attendance at school (excluding the dual-credit courses) in order that high schools can claim the average daily attendance (ADA) for full and half funding. According to their plan, the high school can claim the ADA if for full funding, the students attend high school for 4 hours a day excluding the dual-credit courses; for half funding, students must attend high school 2 hours per day excluding the dual-credit courses. If students are enrolled in fewer than 2 hours per day of instruction, the high school would not be eligible for ADA funding (Texas Education Code, 1995).

If the criteria as proposed by the commissioners are met, then Texas colleges, for example, can enroll students in the dual-credit courses and avoid all appearances, in theory and in fact, of double-dipping. The partnering institutions should, however, devise a plan to monitor the students enrolled in the dual-credit courses on the high school level to ensure that the state's ADA criteria are met.

Dual-Credit Enactment

The statewide education agency can draft language that will regulate the implementation of and parameters of dual-credit programs. In general, language from several states appears to be consistent and includes the following specifics: a permission statement, reference to recognized regional accrediting agencies, eligibility, and academic rigor.

Permission statement. The boards of trustees within the independent school districts are permitted to adopt a policy that allows students to be awarded credit toward high school graduation for completing college-level courses.

Reference to recognized regional accreditation agencies. The courses must be provided only by an institution of higher education that is accredited by one of the following recognized regional accrediting associations:

- Southern Association of Colleges and Schools
- Middle States Association of Colleges and Schools
- New England Association of Schools and Colleges
- North Central Association of Schools and Colleges
- Western Association of Schools and Colleges
- Northwest Association of Schools and Colleges

Eligibility. For a student to be eligible to enroll and be awarded credit toward state graduation requirements, the student must have the approval of the high school principal or other school official as designated by the school district.

Academic rigor. The courses for which credit will be awarded must provide advanced academic instruction beyond, or in greater depth than, the state's requirements for course completion.

Employment of High School Teachers
for Dual-Credit Courses

Teachers should be interviewed before they are hired to teach college-level courses. The process that the college follows when hiring its part-time faculty should also be utilized when hiring dual-credit instructors. Before the faculty member is officially hired, the college's human resources office should have on file the employment application and official transcripts of all faculty members who will be teaching dual-credit courses. Prospective teachers should be required to participate in a college orientation session before they are officially hired to teach the dual-credit courses. Additionally, they should be invited to college-sponsored seminars and workshops that provide information on effective pedagogical strategies including the use of various multimedia techniques that can be used to enhance classroom teaching and student learning.

Student Concerns

Students are somewhat anxious about their first-time experience in college. Therefore, it is of critical importance that all information be carefully explained to students regarding admissions, assessment, placement, registration, and their course of study. If assessment tests will be required, students should be advised beforehand about how to prepare for the tests and the scores that will be required for academic placement. Additionally, enrollment fees and the specific documents that students must bring with them on registration day must be carefully explained. How much will students be charged for the dual-credit courses? Will the fee structure differ if the agreement allows students to take the course at the college location versus the high school site during the regular school day? Students should be told what they will be charged and how they must pay in an effort to eliminate potential problems. The school administration should not wait until the day of registration to sort out these crucial matters.

Orientation Sessions for Faculty and Students

Before the dual-credit classes begin, a series of orientation sessions (one for faculty and one for students and their parents) should be held. Each orientation session should address the purpose of the dual-credit program, the college and high school procedures for enrolling students, the guidelines that will govern students' participation in and continuance in the program, and any additional pertinent information.

College and high school faculty, counselors, and school administrators should participate in the orientation sessions. The faculty orientation session should provide, at minimum, the following:

- Information regarding the faculty member's role as a dual-credit instructor
- Information regarding counseling and advisement for students
- Information about who to contact at the college regarding special issues or questions
- High school and college policies and procedures
- The faculty handbook
- Important contacts at both the high school and college, and their telephone numbers
- High school and college calendars
- Information about assessment and placement of high school students
- Information to prepare new students for the dual-credit program
- Syllabi, textbooks, and reading lists for the course
- Special dates of seminars and programs that faculty should attend
- Other important dates—such as due dates for grades and final reports
- Procedures for evaluating faculty performance

If parents are invited to a special orientation session for students, school personnel should be sensitive to them as a unique audience and as a prospective advocate for the school district and community college. In any event, the orientation session for students is also an appropriate forum to

- Disseminate information regarding procedures that will be followed to enroll students
- Explain the qualifications that (according to state legislation and college policy) will be used for student admission to dual-credit programs
- Explain the placement tests that students must take and entry-level performance required for academic placement
- Tell students the dates on which they will be allowed to register (and the final dates on which they may drop the course)
- Explain the fee amounts that will be charged for courses, give them dates to pay fees and method of payment, and tell them which office will collect the fees
- Provide the important school calendar dates
- Describe the kinds of student services (e.g., learning centers, counseling, and tutorial assistance) that are available to dual-credit students
- Provide the important telephone numbers for community college offices (e.g., registrar, dean's office, counseling office, library, learning center)
- Explain the opportunity students will be given to evaluate the effectiveness of the dual-credit instructional program

The orientation sessions should also be an opportunity for students, high school faculty, and interested parents to ask questions of the college and high school personnel about who will be involved in the dual-credit program. Questions regarding the course content, evaluation of instruction, and grading scales should be a part of the discussion.

If the classes are taught at the high school site, the high school might be expected to share office space and equipment (e.g., photocopiers and facsimile machine) in order to support the college course. The expense related to the particular costs can be negotiated between the two institutions and payment method can be a part of the agreement.

Dual-Credit Classes via Distance Learning

With the increasing availability of technology at high schools and colleges, high school students will be able to complete dual-credit courses via distance learning. The procedures for registration and other enrollment particulars will be the same as those for regular dual-credit classes. There will, however, be a need to closely monitor student performance when utilizing this type of delivery mode. The convenience afforded is that the distance learning configurations will allow high school students to remain at their home sites and receive their college-level instruction via different modalities: computer modem, print, cable, video, or audio. Nevertheless, the students must have access to the same types of institutional support services from the college as do the students who are enrolled in the traditional classroom.

Specific issues regarding the delivery of dual-credit instruction need to be addressed. The following are some of the issues that participating institutions must consider:

- How will the distance education dual-credit courses be monitored for quality?
- How will tests be proctored?
- How will students have access to library services?
- How will students have access to counseling and a range of student services?
- How will students' textbooks, syllabi, and other required course materials be provided?
- How will students be tracked to monitor outcomes and attrition?
- How will distance education students have access to resources for class sessions and course work that they missed?
- How will distance education students make up their missed course work?
- How will students be able to have interaction with their instructors and their peers?

Some school districts have implemented the multipoint inter-active television capacity to maximize student-to-student inter-action. Also, students have Internet access as well as faxes to com-municate with their instructors and their peers. A hotline has also been installed in some districts and an 800 telephone number is available in others to provide communication to students who enroll in distance education courses from other locales or other countries. Questions related to access and quality must, of necessity, be ad-dressed. A collaborative planning team from both institutions could facilitate the design, development, and implementation of a distance education program that would address the specific needs of both groups (high schools and colleges) to partner and simultaneously provide quality education via distance modalities.

Dual-Credit Partnerships With Private Institutions and Charter Schools

The process for implementing dual credit in private institutions is somewhat similar to the process for implementation in public schools. In a review of private institutions and in interviews with the private school administration, the school principal was often found to be the final approval authority. Only occasionally did some pri-vate school boards review educational agreements. Nevertheless, it is recommended that prior to implementation, board approval be sought on all dual-credit arrangements, public and private.

Some private institutions are eager to form partnerships with community colleges for dual-credit programs, particularly if the pro-grams are of high quality and the course work is challenging. Be-cause private institutions do not monitor average daily attendance (ADA) for statewide funding, there is no conflict of potential double-dipping. The community college, however, would need to follow the guidelines as indicated in their regional accrediting agency's criteria relative to faculty credentials and curricular matters. All statewide procedures that allow the college to teach courses at new locations must be reviewed and submitted to the state in order that new in-structional locations be approved for student contact-hour funding.

The same procedure that applies to public high schools applies to Open Enrollment Charter Schools, one of the three types of charter schools approved by the 74th Texas Legislature to operate in Texas. (The other two types are the Home-Rule School District Charter School and the Campus or Campus Program Charter School). The Open Enrollment Charter Schools operate, in principle, in very similar ways to public schools. Open Enrollment Charter Schools, like public schools, are entitled to state funding. They are also entitled to tuition—which is paid by the school district in which the student resides. Open Enrollment Charter Schools are eligible for ADA funding, the procedures that apply to public schools must also apply regarding ways to monitor student enrollments to avoid double-dipping.

If the Open Enrollment Charter School operates in a given school district's facility, that district's board of trustees would be the local approval authority for the dual-credit agreement. If, on the other hand, the charter school is private, is nonprofit, and does not operate in a district-owned facility, the board of the private institution would be the approval authority for the dual-credit agreement—the same as with all other private schools.

Dual Credit and the Educational Purists

Some academicians have remained narrow-minded about dual-credit programs, and for that matter, any form of accelerated programs of learning. Their arguments are steeped in traditionalist thinking. The prevailing attitude among many of them is that college and high school should be separate experiences. In effect, they maintain that high school and college should be separated by discrete variables that regulate students' admission based upon time (the amount of time spent in school) and age (the age of the student). Persons who subscribe to this point of view are called educational purists. They fear that the fusion of high school and college in an academic partnership arrangement weakens standards. The educational purists ask familiar sounding questions: "Why are these students in such a hurry to get through school, anyway?" "What is their rush?" Beyond doubt, the institutions' academic areas have been the least receptive and enthusiastic, initially, to embrace dual credit. Fortunately, the resistance diminishes once the academicians fully understand the philosophy and mission of dual credit, its significance, and the quality control standards that must be a part of every successful program. Dual-credit programs that are data driven help to provide accountability measures and, ultimately, alleviate questions about the quality of the programs.

In any event, society has changed so radically that it is incomprehensible to some why anyone would want to stay on the "slow track," educationally speaking. It is a given that the information technology age and the widespread use of automation demand that institutions modify how they function in order to remain competitive. Technology also affects students and the manner in which they learn. Research data show that many students do not feel challenged by the traditional educational system; thus they drop out. In most conventional settings, students are tested, grouped into artificial categories, and channeled through the educational system at the same rate. How can all these ills be corrected? Given the fact that students learn at different rates and in different ways, it seems obvious that educational programs should be designed to accommodate individual differences, and dual credit is one such effective program.

Entry and exit points are essential in any educational program. Thus, if students are fundamentally capable, based on academic readiness, to pursue higher levels of study, then they should not be retained in a course or restricted to a curriculum sequence as a matter of standard practice. Instead, the students should be challenged and allowed to progress at their own pace. In the long run, this type of philosophy, when articulated, will be liberating to the total educational community and will ultimately benefit a larger percentage of the student population.

Reference Glossary

Articulation. A process, often used in technical programs, that links educational institutions and experiences to assist students in their transition from one level of education to the next without delays or duplications in learning.

Campus or Campus Program Charter School. This type of charter school is established if the governing body of a home-rule district grants a charter to the teachers and the students' parents of a given campus.

Charter schools. As an alternative to operating under a state education code, independent school districts may choose to operate as charter schools that fall into one of three classes: Home-Rule School District Charter Schools, Campus or Campus Program Charter Schools, and Open Enrollment Charter Schools.

Competencies. A set of performance criteria (skills, knowledge, attitudes, performance levels) upon which students are evaluated.

Discipline team. Members of a subject area from high school and college who meet on a periodic basis to review, discuss, and draft recommendations on curricular matters. Discipline teams are formed by selecting faculty who teach in the same disciplines (e.g., math, English, or drafting).

Dual-Credit Course Analysis Worksheet. This worksheet is a guide that may be used in work sessions to identify common course competencies and objectives before courses are recommended for dual credit.

Essential elements. A list of core course objectives, as identified by a state's board of higher education, that high school students must meet.

Home-Rule Charter School. This type of charter school is subject to federal and state laws governing school districts and is subject to a state education code only if specified in the approved agreement. The home-rule charter has taxing authority and virtually the same powers as other districts.

Objectives. Statements that indicate what students are expected to know or to have learned upon completion of a course or a lesson.

Open Enrollment Charter School. This type of charter school is, in effect, considered to be a public school because it is eligible for state funding. It is also eligible to receive tuition from the districts in which students reside.

Tech prep. Tech prep is defined by the Tech Prep Education Act (Title IIIE) as a combined secondary and postsecondary education program that leads to an associate degree or 2-year certificate; provides technical preparation in at least one field of engineering technology, applied science, mechanical, industrial, or practical art or trade, or agriculture, health, or business; builds student competence in mathematics, science, and communication (including applied academics) through a sequence of learning; and leads to placement in employment.

Time-shortened degrees. Degrees that include competencies that are mastered on the secondary level and are applied to the same competencies at the college without the unnecessary duplication of time and effort.

3

Implementing Dual Credit in Certificate and Degree Programs

Two-year institutions have a standard core of academic courses that facilitates students' completion of an Associate in Arts (A.A.) or an Associate in Science (A.S.) degree. Either of these degrees allows students to transfer to a senior-level institution to complete the 4-year degree in the major field. Another option for students, however, is the Associate in Applied Science (A.A.S.) degree, specifically in the technical area, which has a general education requirement of 15 semester–credit hours. All general education courses are in the academic area and could be eligible for dual credit if secondary and postsecondary competencies correlate. Additionally, certificate programs are available for students who would like to quickly gain competencies that will ready them for employment. Certificate programs are largely composed of technical courses; nevertheless, those courses can also, after appropriate review and approval, be offered for dual credit. Many students seek pathways to a career or a 2- or 4-year degree via a time-shortened degree program. Dual credit helps students achieve this objective.

A survey of high school and community college dual-credit programs shows that the dual-credit programs are effective: Students achieve at the same level of competency as those students who are enrolled in the regular college programs and are more inclined to complete their degree or career objective because of their early exposure to a nonthreatening college experience. The "seat time" that students heretofore spent is no longer an issue because of their progressive movement toward their educational or career objective, and the cost to taxpayers is reduced as a result of the more thoughtful and efficient process to education.

Without doubt, dual credit should also be common practice between community colleges and senior universities. That practice has not occurred on a wide scale either, because of a variety of reasons— largely turf protection and resistance to new methodologies. Articulation agreements, however, have been formed between institutions, but those have not been sufficient to address the problems that occur when students attempt to transfer. Perhaps on the postsecondary education level, legislative mandates, which have occurred in some states, will result in a more student-oriented, less costly, time-shortened pathway to a quality higher education for more students. The following is a discussion on how dual-credit initiatives prepare college prep and tech prep students for college transfer, terminal degrees, and the workforce.

Dual Credit, Tech Prep, and the Workforce

The combination of dual-credit initiatives and tech prep educational programs can prepare students to be well trained for the workforce. Although dual credit is considered a college prep initiative, a shift in the paradigm illustrates how tech prep students can also benefit, practically, from general academic curricula that incorporate workplace readiness skills and competencies. For example, some colleges are required by state mandates to incorporate what is known as SCANS Skills and Competencies (for Secretary's Commission on Achieving Necessary Skills) into the general academic curricula. Other postsecondary institutions have recognized the necessity for applied academics and have, by choice, developed revised curricula that allow students to experience the practical application of what they are learning. Thus students who enroll in the general academic dual-credit courses are equipped with a general core of knowledge as well as workplace readiness skills, and they are hence more well prepared for life. Those students are equally well equipped to enter a university parallel program, enroll in a certificate or technical degree program, or enter the workplace. When matching competencies, especially for tech prep students, discipline teams should evaluate whether SCANS Skills and Competencies are active parts of the curricula for the course.

The following are examples that show the core courses in most associate degree programs. As a practice exercise, review the list, and then review the college catalog, course list, and course objectives from community colleges to determine which courses might correlate with the essential elements of the school district. After becoming familiar with the course offerings, the school administrator should plan a meeting with the neighboring institution's team to begin discussions about a dual-credit partnership.

As a reminder, regionally accredited community colleges are generally authorized to offer certificates and A.A., A.S., and A.A.S. degrees. Below is a discussion of each type of degree and its application to the dual-credit process.

Associate in Arts Degree

The A.A. degree applies to programs in the humanities, social sciences, and the arts. Students who enroll in A.A. degree programs generally plan to transfer to a 4-year institution. At most 2-year postsecondary institutions, the A.A. degree consists of a number of core courses that students must complete.

Dual credit is a viable option in most subject areas. Conceivably, as you see in Table 3.1, 18–24 semester-credit hours from this list of core courses could be dual-credit courses. Compare the college's and high school's objectives and competencies to determine if there is a match. Technically, if the essential elements that the state's board of education has for a specific high school course match the course objectives or competencies that a postsecondary institution has for the same course, then that course can be offered for dual credit. An example of essential elements and the cross-match of essential elements and course objectives was discussed in Chapter 2.

Associate in Science Degree

The A.S. degree is awarded for courses of study in mathematics and the natural sciences, as well as in the behavioral and social sciences. The A.S. degree applies typically to degrees in engineering,

In effect, the tech prep student is the counterpart to the academic college prep student.

The difference results from the students' career or educational pathways. A Tech Prep A.A.S. degree in any technical subject requires a general academic core. Either or all of those core courses could be dual-credit courses that would apply in a degree program. Table 3.3 shows a checklist of an A.A.S. degree that includes a dual-credit and articulated-credit component. This option helps the technical student fulfill the requirements for a certificate or a degree.

Institutions will have varying numbers of semester–credit hours that can be awarded for dual credit. Table 3.3 illustrates the different possible configurations. The articulation model, which is really quite similar in many ways, will be discussed in Chapter 6.

Certificates

Many certificates are a part of a degree program. Thus the process that is used to develop a competency analysis for a degree may also be used to develop a competency analysis for a certificate. Because many technical programs have multiple exit points at which students can complete hours for a certificate that will render them qualified in a specific subarea of a technical program, students can earn the certificate and return later to complete the actual A.A.S. degree program.

Annual Course Inventory

On an annual basis, the school district and the community college should meet to determine the recommended course inventory that will be offered for dual credit. Based upon changing standards and emphases, the list should be continuously under review and periodically revised. Also, courses that are offered via distance education should be included on the inventory for tracking and accountability purposes. Table 3.4 shows an example of the course categories to include on an inventory.

TABLE 3.3 Associate in Applied Science Degree Plan in Technical Communication (Excerpt From Degree Plan)[a]

	Semester hours	Dual-credit option	Articulation option
Required academic core			
Composition I	3	3 hours possible	
Composition II	3	3 hours possible	
Intro to psychology	3		
College algebra	3	3 hours possible	
Business and professional speaking	3		
Major area core			
Intro to desktop publishing	3		3 hours possible
Technical composition	3		3 hours possible
Text processing (Mac)	3		
Text processing (IBM)	3		
Tech writing on microcomputers	3		
Proposal writing	3		
Advanced copyediting	3		

(continued)

TABLE 3.3 Continued

	Semester hours	Dual-credit option	Articulation option
Required courses			
Lab/competency in grammar	3		
Business English	3	3 hours possible	
Intro to computer science technology	3		
Computer-aided drafting	3		
Electives			
Technical elective	3		3 hours possible
Technical elective	3		
Technical elective	3		
Total hours:	57	12 hours possible	9 hours possible

a. Dual-credit possibilities as identified by one community college studied.

Districtwide Forum on Dual Credit

Upon successful implementation of the dual-credit process, a districtwide forum on dual credit should be held, and members of various stakeholder groups should be invited to hear about the dual-credit initiative and to offer feedback. The forum, in addition to being informative, should allow for discovery—to determine what is needed from the state to further enhance the process. In planning for the forum, some of the following ideas might be helpful.

TABLE 3.4 Dual-Credit Course Inventory

The following _____ Community College courses are approved for dual high school and college credit in the _____ school district. These courses can be applied at any school throughout the school district as high school graduation credit and may be used as transfer credits to other colleges and universities. The course approval inventory should be reviewed by the instructional administration (both at the high school and the college) and recommended to the superintendent of the school district and to the president or chancellor of the college on an annual basis as the dual-credit agreement is updated. (A sample dual-credit agreement is provided in Chapter 5.)

Complete the following areas for records and distribution.

Academic year: _____

List the specific academic and technical subjects and the modes of instructional delivery. (This model is for illustrative purposes.)

Discipline/courses	Mode of delivery	Responsible agent
The humanities, fine arts, and applied arts courses		
Mathematics/science courses		
Social and behavioral science courses		
Computer science		
Technical courses		
Other		
Date for next inventory update: _____		

- Invite state officials from the coordinating board and the state education agency to discuss their agency's perspectives about dual credit.
- Invite state legislators who serve on the state finance and appropriations committees to attend the forum, listen to dis-

cussions about the partnership, and share the legislature's perspectives on funding of cost-saving educational initiatives.

- Invite faculty and administrators who are effectively delivering dual-credit programs to briefly present the types of programs they have under way in academic and technical areas.
- Invite a school district official to share the district's perspectives about the partnership.
- Invite a college administrator to share the college's perspectives about the partnership.
- Invite superintendents, school principals, and other community college personnel from the region to attend the forum, listen to the discussion, share insights and perspectives, participate in a question-and-answer session, and learn new ideas that can be implemented in the respective districts.

Reference Glossary

Academic core. A standard set of general academic courses, as identified by the college, that all degree-seeking students must take. The core constitutes a breadth of knowledge acquired from several discipline areas: the humanities; fine and applied arts; mathematics, science, and technology; and social and behavioral sciences.

Articulated credit. Transfer credit that results from matching course competencies in the technical field and applying the credit from high school to college-level work.

4

Evaluating
Program Effectiveness

Dual-credit programs should be evaluated to assess the levels of programmatic and instructional effectiveness. Evaluation data equip the institution to (a) refine the dual-credit program based on student outcome measures and (b) develop objective data analyses that can be used when responding to various constituent groups, including accrediting agencies, state legislators, and others about the quality and effectiveness of the dual-credit program. Assessment plans should evaluate the following: student retention, student performance measures via grade distribution reports, student transfer to postsecondary institutions upon graduation, and long-term student tracking. Additional critical data include attitudinal indicators and perceptual indicators, which will have a direct influence upon the attitudes of students, teachers, and administrators concerning dual-credit programs.

The instruments included at the end of this chapter may be copied and used to gather qualitative data. First, in workshop settings, administrators can distribute the Teacher-Student Interaction (TSI) Instrument to teachers. The TSI has been tested for validity and reliability and has been successfully used since 1979. The TSI scale is used as a measure to identify the category of teacher attitudes. Five profile categories are possible. The categories range from the most conservative and frequently insecure posture of being highly alienated from others and having low self-esteem to the ultimate category of being an open-minded, free-thinking, and accepting person as concerns individual, cultural, and ethnic differences. Ford (1979) found that the positive attitudes of teachers in classroom settings are essential for maximum effectiveness with students. Frequently, the teacher's attitude is the factor that influences the degree of student interest in the course or subject matter. Teachers' attitudes also frequently influence student performance.

Some teachers may not be aware of their disparate treatment of students. The biases may emerge from the teacher's personal gender or ethnic group experiences, the teacher's perceptions about gender and ethnic groups, society's treatment of certain groups, or the practices within a particular school or community setting. Teachers should seek greater self-awareness and examine the ultimate effect of their own attitudes and behaviors on students.

The TSI Instrument has been modified to incorporate views of teachers about students in dual-credit programs. Interviews with administrators at schools where dual credit is in place indicate that very few ethnic minority and high-risk students qualify for the program. This finding is worth investigation. Additional steps must be taken to ensure that all students are given an opportunity to enhance their learning and set a course for future success.

The TSI Instrument should be completed by instructors, preferably during inservice workshops. During the workshops, instructors will have an opportunity to complete the instrument in a nonthreatening setting, get feedback to their responses, and discuss ways to enhance their personal effectiveness in working with diverse groups of students and in diverse teaching environments.

As an alternative, instructors may decide to respond to the instrument in private to ascertain their personal profile in teacher–student interaction. This approach is acceptable but less effective because, to some degree, it is the actual discussion of the responses that fosters instructor awareness and heightened sensitivity to a diverse audience. The dynamics of the open discussion group process frequently result in conversion experiences that have long-term, positive benefits for students.

In the end analysis, regardless of the process for administering the instrument (individual or group), the instructors' responses will provide meaningful information that can be used in a constructive, nonpunitive manner to enhance teaching and learning.

The second instrument included in this study focuses on questions that students should be asked regarding their dual-credit experience. That instrument is the Student Perception Inventory (SPI) of dual-credit programs. The SPI was developed in 1996, specifically to be administered to dual-credit students. Feedback from students provides meaningful information for evaluating teacher-student interaction and programmatic effectiveness. Both instruments provide meaningful data to help school districts assess the strengths and weaknesses of dual-credit programs and to identify areas of concern. The end result is enhanced quality within instructional programs.

The TSI should be administered to faculty in workshop settings, whereas the SPI should be administered to students midway through the semester of a dual-credit course. On the other hand, the Administrative Evaluation Instrument (the third component of the evaluation process) is an observation tool, and it can be administered at any point in the semester. It can be used by administrators who observe instructors of dual-credit classes. The administrative evaluation should be conducted by a department head or dean, partially during the classroom observation process and, finally, in consultation with the instructor. When all data—quantitative and qualitative—are collected, compiled, and evaluated, the data analysis report, with an accompanying list of recommendations, should be distributed to faculty and administrators within the high school and college; shared with the partnering institution; and distributed to school board members, legislators, the parent-teacher association, and other policymakers and stakeholder groups.

Reference Glossary

Administrative Evaluation Instrument. This assessment, developed in 1996, is constructed to be used in classroom observation and individualized conferences with dual-credit instructors.

High-risk students. A category of students who, based on previous school attendance patterns, school performance records, and/or socioeconomic status, might be likely candidates to drop out of school.

Student Perception Inventory (SPI). A survey instrument developed in 1996 that provides one set of student data on the effectiveness of dual-credit educational programs.

Teacher–Student Interaction (TSI) Instrument. A survey instrument developed in 1979 that identifies teachers' levels of effectiveness in working with diverse student populations.

Teacher–Student Interaction (TSI) Instrument

Scale

0 = strongly agree
1 = agree
2 = borderline
3 = disagree
4 = strongly disagree

Directions: Please circle the number that indicates your response to each statement.

1. As a minority in this country, I (would) feel very self-conscious about my ethnic identity.

0   1   2   3   4

2. I can only develop personal relationships and ties with persons who hold similar values to mine.

0   1   2   3   4

3. The fact that white ethnic groups have more powerful positions than minorities illustrates the inherent superiority of whites.

0   1   2   3   4

4. If I were a minority administrator in the schools today, I would pattern all of my behaviors after those of white administrators.

0   1   2   3   4

5. When I meet people who have beliefs that are similar to mine, I trust them implicitly.

0   1   2   3   4

6. I have a tendency to trust students of my ethnic group more than I trust those of other ethnic groups.

0   1   2   3   4

7. I try to avoid people who have a different value system from my own.

0   1   2   3   4

8. People should be deeply sensitive to others' opinions of them.

0   1   2   3   4

9. People should strive to become more Americanized.

0   1   2   3   4

10. I feel most secure when I am around persons who are of the same gender as I.

0   1   2   3   4

11. Because of the way that I was raised, I believe that whites are superior, and other groups are inferior.

0   1   2   3   4

12. I automatically extend special privileges to students of my ethnic group.

0   1   2   3   4

13. I feel "edgy" when I socialize with people who are different.

0   1   2   3   4

14. A student's ethnic group influences my behavior toward him or her more than anything else.

0   1   2   3   4

15. Schools should not be required to address cultural diversity issues.

0   1   2   3   4

16. When I am offended by an ethnic minority, I generalize the behavior to persons of that group.

0   1   2   3   4

17. In order to be accepted by other ethnic groups, I frequently change my behavior.

0   1   2   3   4

18. Students are better pupils if they are taught by persons of their own ethnic group.

0   1   2   3   4

19. When students come to school, they should leave their ethnic identities at home.

0   1   2   3   4

20. If I had a choice, I would prefer working only with socio-economically privileged persons.

0   1   2   3   4

21. When I see a group of minorities together, I automatically become frightened.

0   1   2   3   4

22. I feel tense and uptight when I have to work closely with students and teachers who are of a different ethnic group.

0   1   2   3   4

23. I believe that some ethnic groups have no standards to distinguish between right and wrong.

0   1   2   3   4

24. Cultural and ethnic group differences should not be discussed among students in school.

0   1   2   3   4

25. I prefer isolating myself from everyone.

0   1   2   3   4

26. People should have intimate associations with persons of their ethnic group ONLY.

0   1   2   3   4

27. I have a low tolerance level for anyone who is different from me.

0   1   2   3   4

28. All students should be required to speak English at school.

0   1   2   3   4

29. Because of my upbringing, I naturally expect males to perform much better in school than females.

0   1   2   3   4

Comments:

Developed by Dr. Margaret L. Ford, 1996. The Likert approach to attitude scale construction and scoring is used to establish individual and/or group profiles.

Student Perception Inventory (SPI)
of the Effectiveness of Dual-Credit Programs

Scale

0 = no knowledge
1 = strongly disagree
2 = disagree
3 = agree
4 = strongly agree

Section 1 of this instrument is to be completed by all dual-credit students.

Section 1—General

Directions: Please circle the number that indicates your response to each statement.

1. The instructor responds quickly to students' requests for explanations and information.

0   1   2   3   4

2. The instructor relates to students in an appropriate manner.

0   1   2   3   4

3. The teacher uses appropriate and easy-to-understand language and terminology to explain information.

0   1   2   3   4

4. All students who meet the eligibility criteria should be encouraged to take dual-credit courses.

0   1   2   3   4

5. The dual-credit experience makes me feel more motivated to do well in school, graduate from high school, and pursue a college degree.

0   1   2   3   4

6. I will recommend dual-credit courses to my friends.

0   1   2   3   4

7. Access to the college's learning resource center, counselors, and educational support services helps me acclimate more easily to a college environment.

0   1   2   3   4

8. I believe students will perform better in dual-credit programs if they have a college orientation that is tailored specifically for the high school dual-credit student before admission to college-credit courses.

0   1   2   3   4

9. The opportunity to take dual-credit courses as a high school student will help to build my self-confidence prior to full-time college enrollment.

0   1   2   3   4

10. My instructor provided me with detailed information about the goals and requirements of each course, the course content, the methods of evaluation, and where I can get various educational support services.

0   1   2   3   4

11. I enrolled in dual-credit classes because I wanted to be academically challenged by the subject matter, the instructor, and my peers.

0   1   2   3   4

12. I believe that I have the same access to college advisement and counseling as the regular college students on the college campus.

0   1   2   3   4

13. Dual-credit offerings during the senior year of high school help to offset "senioritis."

0   1   2   3   4

Section 2 of this instrument is to be completed by high school students who are taking dual-credit courses that are taught by high school teachers who teach full-time at the high school.

Section 2—High School Instructor Teaching Dual-Credit Courses

Directions: Please circle the number that indicates your response to each statement.

14. I like the fact that my high school teacher, who meets all college-level qualifications, teaches the dual-credit high school and college course.

0   1   2   3   4

15. My dual-credit course is academically challenging and is taught at a higher level than high school courses.

0   1   2   3   4

16. Taking dual-credit courses as a high school student will help me to be more confident when I enroll in college on a full-time basis.

0   1   2   3   4

17. Parental influence is what led me to enroll in dual-credit courses.

0   1   2   3   4

Section 3 should be completed by the high school students who are taking dual-credit distance education courses (via computer modem, video, cable, etc.).

Section 3—Distance Education

Directions: Please circle the number that indicates your response to each statement.

18. I am taking a dual-credit course via distance education, and I think the course is academically challenging and of high quality.

0   1   2   3   4

19. Distance education is an ideal way to earn a diploma and a degree.

0   1   2   3   4

20. I have not had difficulty gaining access to college counselors and to college library resources via electronic means in my distance education courses.

0   1   2   3   4

Comments:

Developed by Dr. Margaret L. Ford, 1996. The Likert approach to attitude scale construction and scoring is used to establish individual and/or group profiles.

Administrative Evaluation Instrument of
Teaching Effectiveness in Dual-Credit Classes

0 = strongly disagree
1 = disagree
2 = borderline
3 = agree
4 = strongly agree

Directions: Please circle the number that indicates your response to each statement.

1. The instructor uses the college-level textbooks and syllabi that meet all standards of the college.

0   1   2   3   4

2. The instructor demonstrates skill in getting students to participate actively in their learning.

0   1   2   3   4

3. The instructor uses a variety of teaching and evaluation strategies.

0   1   2   3   4

4. The instructor organizes and presents subject matter effectively.

0   1   2   3   4

5. The instructor encourages students to think critically.

0   1   2   3   4

6. The instructor is well prepared for class.

0   1   2   3   4

7. The instructor keeps accurate records of student performance.

0   1   2   3   4

8. The instructor meets the class as scheduled, including beginning and ending class on time.

0   1   2   3   4

9. The instructor teaches subject matter that is consistent with the course.

0   1   2   3   4

10. The instructor works cooperatively with colleagues and staff.

0   1   2   3   4

11. The instructor maintains appropriate communication with his or her supervisor.

0   1   2   3   4

12. The instructor returns graded materials to students in a timely manner.

0   1   2   3   4

13. The instructor dresses appropriately for class.

0   1   2   3   4

14. The instructor demonstrates concern for all students in the class.

0   1   2   3   4

Comments:

Developed by Dr. Margaret L. Ford, 1996. The Likert approach to attitude scale construction and scoring is used to establish individual and/or group profiles.

5

Developing Agreements
Between Institutions:
An Annotated Sample

This chapter provides an annotated sample of a dual-credit agreement. After having read previous chapters, it is clear that in most states, dual-credit partnerships must first be authorized by the state legislature. The state's board of education and its commission on higher education must establish rules and guidelines for regulating dual-credit programs. After rules are in place, local school districts will be able to proceed with planning the program. Finally, the high school and college administrations should seek approval from their boards of trustees to implement the innovative partnership. The following is an annotated sample of key points that should be addressed in the dual-credit agreements.

Sample Annotated Dual-Credit Agreement

I. Agreement Statement

AGREEMENT made this _____ day of _____ , 19_____ , between the Board of Trustees of _____ Community College and _____ Independent School District.

Explanation: The Agreement Statement indicates the institutions' willingness to participate in the dual-credit partnership.

II. Purpose

This dual-credit agreement is designed to award college credit to students who successfully complete college-level courses. For the purposes of this agreement, dual credit is an agreement, entered into by the _____ Community College and the _____ Independent School District, that common objectives and competencies exist between the two entities. With a review of the course objectives and competencies, students who have passed all high school competency tests are eligible and will be allowed to enroll in college-level courses based upon the terms and conditions listed below.

Explanation: The Purpose Statement clarifies the intent of the partnership for the board and the partnering institutions.

III. Procedural Steps in the Agreement Process

The following section of the agreement pertains to all procedural matters regarding the dual-credit process. An explanation follows each procedural step as further clarifying information for the reader.

1. All students who enroll must be tested with the **(name of test)** college admission's test. The college will send a testing specialist to the high school site to test the students for placement. A registration technician will also be sent from the college to register all eligible students for the college-level course(s).

Explanation: Some colleges do not administer placement tests. Others only administer placement tests in single-discipline subjects (reading, writing, or math areas). The college should be consistent in the tests that are used for placing all students who seek admission, irrespective of whether the tests are for regular college-level students or for dual-credit students. Because all students do not necessarily have equal access to transportation, it is recommended that all testing specialists as well as registration specialists be sent to the high school site to enroll students for classes.

2. Students who are enrolled in dual-credit courses will not be permitted to take more than 6 semester–credit hours per semester (fall, spring, and summer) for dual credit. In essence, a high school student may complete 18 semester–credit hours of transferable college work in one calendar year.

Explanation: In an effort to promote student success, students should be monitored to determine the maximum number of dual-credit hours that are permissible per semester. Under ordinary circumstances, no student should be permitted to enroll in more than 6 semester–credit hours per semester. The high school students still have high school demands, plus they have other extracurricular activities to which they must attend without distraction. Because most high schools are closed for the summer, special permission should be sought for high school students to enroll at the college for dual-credit courses.

3. Counseling services will be made available to students who are enrolled in dual-credit courses, and educational plans will be completed for all students by the time they complete **(specify the number of hours)** number of credit hours of college-level work.

Explanation: High school and college counseling services will be available to students. A routine practice will be established for college counselors to be available to dual-credit high school students. Additionally, an educational plan should be established for students by the time they complete 12 semester–credit hours in order to help students get focused with regard to their college goals. (Research data show that students are more successful in college and are more inclined to complete their college degrees if they are focused and have a clear goal or objective in mind.) The college intends to help students move toward their educational and career goals.

4. All students who take the college-level courses must take the **(name the test)** test upon completing **(specify the number of hours)** semester hours of college-level work.

Explanation: Many states require students to take legislatively mandated competency tests at a specific point in their educational plan. Students are required to pass the tests before they graduate.

5. Students must register or enroll in the college course.

Explanation: The only way that students can get dual credit for high school and college work is that they must be registered or enrolled in the college course. There are some fine shades of differences between dual credit and dual enrollment. Many states use the terms interchangeably. The differences are highlighted below:

- Dual credit occurs when a student receives credit at two institutions for all work completed.

- Dual enrollment occurs when a student is enrolled at two institutions. Credit may or may not be awarded for work that is completed.

6. Students will pay the tuition and building-use fee for the college-level course.

Explanation: This item is negotiable. If the student is taking the course at the high school, the agreement may exempt the student from having to pay the building-use fee. This is an item that should be agreed upon early in the discussions.

7. All courses will be identified on the transcript as the regular college-level course. No designation will be used to indicate that the dual-credit courses were taken while the student was still in high school.

Explanation: Some senior-level institutions may be less inclined to accept course credit and more inclined to question the rigor of the course if they associate it with work completed while the student was still in high school. Therefore, this item is very important to include in the agreement to avoid stigmatizing the courses, the students, or the institutions.

8. High school teachers will teach the dual-credit courses only if they meet the educational and professional preparation requirements of the community college, which include compliance with the accrediting agencies and the state guidelines for licensing.

Explanation: For faculty to teach the transferable courses, those faculty members must meet all college-level standards as set by the specific regional accrediting agency that regulates that particular region and as set by the state's rules and guidelines.

9. All students who are performing poorly in the course will be counseled and then dropped from the college-level course in order to avoid establishing a poor college level of performance.

Explanation: The intent of the dual-credit plan is to help students achieve success—not to promote failure. Therefore, it is critical that teachers and counselors work very closely with the high school students to transfer them from the college-level component of the course to the high school component. Thus, although the student would not get credit for the college course, the student would, however, get credit for the high school course.

10. Dual credit will be offered in both the academic and technical areas.

Explanation: Dual credit can be successfully offered in both the academic as well as the technical program areas. The academic component would buttress the college credit attainment for those students who are on the college prep track. Equally important, the tech prep–oriented student can benefit from dual credit. The dual credit could be accumulated in the general academic courses or in the technical areas. This option will provide more alternatives for students who are interested in the Tech Prep Associate's degree who would otherwise be awarded only articulated credit.

11. Courses will be offered on the high school campuses during the regular school day during the fall and spring semesters. Courses will be offered on the college campus during the summer term.

Explanation: During the summer months, most high schools that do not have year-round programs are closed. Yet, it is possible that prior agreements will permit the students to take a specified number of high school courses for dual high school and college credit.

12. College-level textbooks and syllabi must be used as a requirement to fulfill the terms of the dual-credit program.

Explanation: Maintaining college standards is crucial. The standards used are very important to the overall strength of dual-credit programs. In an effort to prepare students who will be educationally competitive, it is essential that the same rigorous college standards be applied and that the same textbooks, syllabi, tests, course outlines, and the like be used irrespective of where (on- or off-campus) or how (regular instruction or distance education) instruction is delivered.

13. The superintendent and college president will annually review the course offerings and will update the list as needed.

Explanation: It is important to annually review the courses, students' performance in the courses, requirements for improving the dual-credit process, identification of other courses that may be added to the dual-credit list, and an identification of courses that may be deleted from the list.

14. The college discipline teams and the high school discipline teams will match competencies and will identify the courses that they would like to recommend via administration to the superintendent and president for dual credit.

Explanation: This should be an ongoing process in which the discipline specialists from both the high school and the college meet on a periodic basis to review changing course requirements, course objectives, course competencies, and the efficacy of the program.

15. College-level department heads, coordinators, or deans will be permitted to visit the high school campus and observe the classes of instructors who are teaching dual-credit courses.

Explanation: Because the course is a college course, the college instructional administrators must have the freedom to visit the classes and provide the same type of administrative oversight as would occur if the class were being conducted at one of the college campuses.

16. All high school faculty who teach the dual-credit courses during the regular school day will be paid their regular salary by the high school. If high school teachers instruct the dual-credit classes, the teachers will also be paid a stipend by the college to teach the courses. The community college, school district, and instructors will agree to a plan that will be consistent with state guidelines and regulations.

Explanation: The state agencies for secondary and postsecondary education must be assured that all financial disbursements will be in accordance with state guidelines.

17. The high school and college boards of trustees will each review and vote for approval or nonapproval of the dual-credit partnership.

Explanation: Board action is critically important, for only the boards can set policies and act as the final authority on institutional matters.

IV. Board Chair and Administrative CEO Signatures

BOARD OF TRUSTEES OF _____
COMMUNITY COLLEGE

By: _____
      Chairman, Board of Trustees

ATTEST: _____

BOARD OF TRUSTEES OF _____

INDEPENDENT SCHOOL DISTRICT

By: _____
       Chairman, Board of Trustees

ATTEST: _____

Explanation: The agreement is not official until it is voted upon and approved by the boards and signed by the board chairs of both institutions.

Reference Glossary

Dual-credit agreement. The dual-credit agreement is a document that is approved by each institution's board of trustees.

Dual-credit course plan. A plan of courses that is proposed for dual credit. The course plan is signed by the chief executive officers and the instructional administration of both institutions.

6

Dual Credit
Versus Articulated Credit

Throughout this work, one focus has been on dual credit as an option for high school students to earn time-shortened degrees. Dual credit results in the following benefits for students:

- An immediate college transcript for courses taken in the academic or technical subject area
- Transferable course credit to postsecondary institutions—not just the one that holds the joint agreement
- Elimination of unnecessary duplication of course work
- Cost savings for the student

Now, attention will be focused on articulated credit as another approach, often used in technical programs, for students who are interested in earning time-shortened degrees. Other fine, established approaches are also used to earn time-shortened degrees, but for the two approaches addressed in this context—dual credit and articulated credit—little information is available that provides a replicable process.

Articulated credit and dual credit are in many ways similar. Both are time-shortened pathways for students to earn a degree or a certificate. Articulation, for example, is a process that (a) coordinates instructional programs and (b) guides student matriculation from high school to the community college in related technical programs without duplicating course work. Articulation requires that course competencies be matched. If the high school and college course competencies are the same, students will be able to take the high school courses and transfer the credit to the local community college with whom the high school holds the joint articulation agreement.

Articulated credit results in the following benefits for students:

- Transfer of technical education credit to the college that holds the joint agreement
- Elimination of unnecessary duplication of course work
- Cost savings for the student

The articulation of occupational and technical programs with secondary schools provides for the award of college credit for competencies achieved at the secondary school. The articulated credit transfers to the college that holds the agreement with the high school.

Elements of an Effective Articulation Process

After a review of articulation processes, it is evident that there are specific components to an effective approach to articulation. The high school and community college administrators should incorporate the following components into their articulation processes.

A clear, comprehensive plan. The plan should include the specific objectives for articulation and a time line for review and evaluation of the articulation process.

Good communication among participants. The participants in the articulation process must feel respected for their knowledge and expertise, and there must be open and clear communication at all times. A single point of contact should be identified with the college and with the school district. All communication should flow through the points of contact of the respective institutions.

Strong and dynamic administrative support. The only effective way that the articulation process will be successful is if it is sanctioned by the top-level administration and if active support (institutional and financial) for the process is genuinely communicated to the members of the team.

Unity toward a common purpose. The clear goals and objectives and the time line of implementation, evaluation, and reporting to constituents will help keep the process focused and unified toward a common purpose.

Academically sound procedures to ensure a reasonable chance for students' success. In planning the sequences of courses for students to take, the advising or counseling component is key to student success. Thus the same procedures that are used for students on the college campus for charting their matriculation process should be used for high school students who are enrolled in the articulated courses.

Emphasis on long-range career planning. The long-range career planning is primarily done to facilitate student success. Thus career counselors play an integral role in advising students about which courses to take toward completion of their educational goals.

An articulation plan should be developed by the school district and community college to determine whether course competencies match. In fact, a process similar to the one used to match competencies and objectives for dual credit may be used for matching technical competencies. Thus the faculty who are involved in articulation discussion teams or discipline teams can do the following:

- Exchange detailed course content documentation as needed
- Discuss course content and how the content can be modified
- Resolve questions about content and achievement levels
- Explore areas in which modification is needed
- Visit classrooms and laboratories in both the high school and college to evaluate whether the classroom and laboratory conditions are consistent with the standards of accrediting or licensing agencies
- Compare course competencies by completing the articulation course competency analysis form

It is important to remember that courses taken by high school students must be a part of the educational plan at the community college. As is the case with dual-credit students, the students must be eligible for admission to the college, and the college must have an official high school transcript on all students who enroll.

The following is a sample articulation agreement that includes recommended steps for the school administration's review and approval.

Articulation Agreement: An Example

AGREEMENT made this _____ day of _____, 199 _____, between the Board of Trustees of _____ Community College and _____ Independent School District.

Purpose

This articulation agreement is designed to award college credit to students who successfully meet all criteria for articulation. For the purposes of this agreement, articulation is an agreement entered into by the _____ Community College and the _____ Independent School District, that common objectives and competencies exist between the two entities. With a review of the course objectives and competencies, credit will be awarded for courses in which objectives and competencies were achieved in the corresponding course.

Agreement

Under this articulation agreement, the following conditions of articulation are hereby set forth:

I. Students

In order that the high school student become eligible for credit by articulation the student must do the following:

- Meet all college admissions requirements and be officially enrolled at the college
- Have an official high school transcript on file with the admissions office
- Initiate an official educational plan with the appropriate counselor at the time of enrollment at the college
- Complete the high school courses for which articulation credit is being requested within 1 year of the request for credit
- Meet all conditions for articulation credit as stated in the specific articulation plan (see the following articulation plan) that covers the requested course(s)

- Successfully complete all exit criteria at the completion of each course for which college credit is being granted
- Successfully complete specified high school course(s)

II. Faculty

The faculty designee responsible for articulated course credit must evaluate the official high school transcript and recommend articulation credit based on the stated conditions in the applicable articulation plan. (The recommendation will be submitted to the appropriate administrators for approval and implementation.)

III. Administration

The college administrators who are responsible for the disciplines included in the articulation agreement must initiate an annual review of the articulation plan with the high school officials to evaluate any changes in competencies, content, or standards.

IV. General Information

As a general practice, the articulation plans must be on file with the admissions office and with the instructional vice president. This agreement is a living document and may be terminated in whole or in part by either party by giving a full 30 days notice in writing to the other party. Such notice shall be sent by certified mail, return receipt requested, to the address of the respective CEO.

With regard to students, such termination shall not commence until the currently enrolled students have completed their respective courses.

V. Signatures

[Note: As with the dual credit agreement, the board chair of the partnering institution should sign the document to make the partnership official.]

BOARD OF TRUSTEES OF _____
COMMUNITY COLLEGE

By: _____
  Chairman, Board of Trustees

ATTEST: _____

BOARD OF TRUSTEES OF _____

INDEPENDENT SCHOOL DISTRICT

By: _____
  Chairman, Board of Trustees

ATTEST: _____

* * *

The following is an example of an articulation plan that provides a process for students to be granted articulated credit under specific conditions of articulation.

Articulation Plan: An Example

Department: _____

Subject Area: _____

Purpose

This process confirms approval of an articulation plan for the courses and programs in the areas listed above between the _____ College and the _____ Independent School District. Articulation approval has been granted in the Articulation Agreement signed by school board officials from the two institutions. This document provides a process for students to be granted credit by articulation under the specific conditions of articulation. The courses that will be articulated are listed below.

Independent School District Course Name and Number

Credits Awarded

College Course Name and Number

Credit Hours Awarded

_____

_____

_____

The conditions of the articulation plan were formulated through meetings with administrators and faculty representatives from both the high school and the college. The plan was based on an agreement to the following areas: evaluation criteria, course content, and exit competencies. Under the articulation agreement, the following conditions of articulation were established:

I. Students

In order that the high school student become eligible for credit by articulation the student must do the following:

- Meet all college admissions requirements and be officially enrolled at the college
- Have an official high school transcript on file with the admissions office
- Initiate an official educational plan with the appropriate counselor at the time of enrollment at the college
- Complete the high school courses for which articulation credit is being requested within 1 year of the request for credit
- Meet all conditions for articulation credit as stated in the specific articulation plan that covers the requested course(s)
- Successfully complete all exit criteria at the completion of each course for which college credit is being granted
- Successfully complete specified high school course(s)

II. Faculty

The faculty designee responsible for articulated course credit will evaluate the official high school transcript and recommend articulation credit based on the stated conditions in the applicable articulation plan. (The recommendation will be submitted to the appropriate administrators for approval and implementation.)

III. Administration

The college administrators who are responsible for the disciplines included in the articulation agreement must initiate an annual review of the articulation plan with the high school officials to evaluate any changes in competencies, content, or standards.

TABLE 6.1 Courses and Credits Available

High school course	College course/credits
Business Computer Application I and Business Computer Applications II	Computer Science 1311: Introduction to Computer Science, 3 semester credits

IV. General Information

As a general practice, the articulation plans must be on file with the admissions office and with the instructional vice president. This agreement is a living document and may be terminated in whole or in part by either party by giving a full 30 days notice in writing to the other party. Such notice shall be sent by certified mail, return receipt requested, to the address of the respective CEO.

With regard to students, such termination shall not commence until the currently enrolled students have completed their respective courses.

V. Articulation Information

Following is information that completes the articulation process: course descriptions of high school and college courses being articulated, exit competencies for courses being articulated for credit, and other supporting materials. Table 6.1 shows an example of two courses for articulation that will be discussed in the following section.

* * *

Course Articulation Exit Competencies: An Example

The exhibit illustrates the exit competencies that students must master to be awarded transfer credit.

Intent

The _____ Community College agrees to award college credit for two Business Computer Applications courses completed at the _____ Independent School District based upon the conditions listed below. Credits may be awarded for the courses provided the listed criteria are met.

Criteria

Students who complete the above high school courses are eligible for articulation credit at _____ College by meeting the following criteria.

1. The student must have a passing grade of B or higher at the completion of Business Computer Applications I and Business Computer Applications II courses at the high school level; textbook selection and faculty qualifications must be consistent with college standards; and students will be required to take the Credit-by-Exam for Computer Science 1311 and will be expected to pass at a rate of 75% or higher.

2. For the articulation of credit to occur, students must enroll at the community college within 2 years after high school graduation and enroll in a certificate or associate degree program containing Computer Science 1311— Introduction to Computer Science.

Signatures

On this date _____ , the signatures of representatives of the respective institutions acknowledge a commitment to effectively accommodate the conditions of the articulation plan that is attached.

_____	_____
Community College	Independent School District
_____	_____
Division Head	Signature/Title
_____	_____
Dean	Signature/Title
_____	_____
Vice President of Instruction	Signature/Title

Configurations of Articulated Credit

There are differing configurations for articulating course credit in the technical education area. With tech prep, for example, designations such as 1+1, 2+1, 2+2, 2+2+2, and 4+2 have become a regular part of the nomenclature. Those patterns refer to ways competencies can be addressed in high school, college, and university levels that will allow students to matriculate through school to ultimately complete the baccalaureate degree. For example, in the vertical articulation process for high schools, course credits are generally transferred from secondary schools to postsecondary institutions. The vertical articulation of courses, for example, allows for the coordination of courses and credits at the levels indicated (secondary and postsecondary) without the unnecessary duplication of course work; ultimately, this process results in time-shortened degrees or certificates. The horizontal articulation process refers to the programmatic transfer of credit either intra- or interinstitutionally. A configuration of the process is included in Table 6.2.

Although the articulation process is an effective tool to help students gain access to college, it is strongly recommended that, whenever possible, students enroll in dual-credit courses. The dual-credit vehicle allows students, academic and technical, more degrees of freedom upon high school graduation.

Staff Requirements

Each institution should consider assigning one person responsibility for articulation and dual-credit agreements. That person can work with the instructional area, counseling area, and partnering institutions to update agreements and articulation plans, file appropriate paperwork in a timely fashion, initiate periodic evaluation of all partnership programs, and maintain all official files of articulation and dual-credit agreements.

TABLE 6.2 Configurations of Articulation

Articulation	High school	College	University
1+1	Senior year	Freshman year	
2+1	Junior/senior years	Freshman year	
2+2	Junior/senior years	Freshman/ sophomore years	
2+2+2	Junior/senior years	Freshman/ sophomore years	Junior/senior years
4+2	Freshman/ sophomore/ junior/senior years	Freshman/ sophomore years	

Reference Glossary

1+1 Program. An articulated postsecondary education program that is offered by community and technical colleges wherein the first year of study is offered by one institution and the second year is offered by a second participating institution that offers the applied associates degree.

2+1 Program. An articulated, competency-based program that links 4 years of secondary school (9–12) with 2 years at a community college and 2 years at a senior-level university.

2+2 Program. An articulated, competency-based program that links 2 years of secondary schoold (11-12) with 1 year at a community college.

2+2+2 Program. An articulated, competency-based program that links a 2+2 program to the last 2 years of higher education and ideally results in a baccalaureate degree.

4+2 Program. An articulated, competency-based program that links 4 years of secondary school (9–12) with 2 years at a community college.

7

Engaging Faculty
in Systemic Change

Articulated credit and dual credit are outstanding vehicles for students to use to access the continuum of learning. The continuum not only leads to time-shortened degrees, but ultimately to a more fulfilling educational experience for students. Frequently, the state requirements for high school courses and the course competencies for college-level courses do not differ greatly. When there is commonality, dual credit should be implemented to avoid repetition and duplication of effort at the secondary and postsecondary levels. This partnership creates a practical and very cost-effective approach to education for students, parents, taxpayers, and the community at large.

Based upon the implementation model in urban and suburban school districts, thus far, and interviews with school district personnel, dual credit unquestionably provides an incentive for high school students to excel. Nationwide, dual-credit offerings are bridging the gap between secondary and postsecondary education. But if dual-credit programs are to be a continued success and if they are to be embraced by educational purists, factors related to quality and efficacy must be addressed. Administrations can support the initiative by utilizing the following methodology to engage faculty in systemic changes in educational partnerships—in this instance, for dual credit.

Methodology for Engaging Faculty
in Systemic Educational Changes

Systemic change should be an institutional effort. Thus administrators, faculty, staff, and students should be involved. The following is an inclusion model for engaging faculty, staff, and students in the systemic change process.

A standing committee, appointed by the chief executive officer of the institution, should evaluate the dual-credit proposal and, via a process of consensus, recommend to the senior administration the extent to which the school should be involved in the initiative. The group should review each of the following issues and develop appropriate strategies in its exploratory process.

Identify mission and purpose. Mission and purpose help lay the foundation for any new initiative. Thus the planning committee should participate in discussions about the mission and the purpose of dual credit and its place in the institution's mission. The committee should define its parameters and how it wants to fulfill its mandate to serve the educational needs of the individual and the community.

Develop an action plan. The dual-credit committee should develop an action plan for the expansion of the institution's mission. The plan should include goals, objectives, time lines, and responsible agents within the institution that will help actualize the plan.

Identify unclear motives. Meetings with members of the school's planning team should identify the specific motivations for the schools' actions. The information should be recorded and distributed to all members of the faculty, staff, and student council and be made available to other interested constituencies.

Identify unknown consequences. The planning team should identify the pros and cons of the mission and the attendant goals and objectives. Discussions should identify all potential consequences of the initiatives and contingency plans that the school can implement.

Sanction the new initiative. Once it is decided that the new initiative will be undertaken, the administrative leadership must convey its unyielding support. The support must be demonstrated in an ongoing, clearly demonstrative manner.

Reaffirm commitment to quality education and high educational standards. The planning team should discuss quality control standards and how they will be maintained. Checkpoints should be established so the planning team can monitor the new initiative for its compliance with high school, college, state, federal, and accrediting agency criteria.

Avoid intimidation of faculty and staff who disagree. Because the planning initiative is a collaborative one, every effort should be made to nurture open communication and feedback. Thus all planning team members should be confident that their comments, if negative and opposed to the administration's, will not result in reprisal.

Determine data assessment procedures. Because accountability is of vital importance, the team should decide how it wants to assess the effectiveness of the new initiative. In any event, it is essential that the new initiative be data driven to determine its strengths, weaknesses, and overall effectiveness in achieving outcomes.

Foster awareness of and responsiveness to external controls. On the new initiative, as with any program, administrators must be willing to provide status reports to various constituencies. Sensitivity to the constituent group's needs will help facilitate support of the larger educational program and of the school. The planning team can assist in providing meaningful information to key constituent groups.

Schedule program reviews. On an annual basis, programs should be reviewed for modification, continuation, or termination. The committee should agree to any major changes that occur. Appropriate actions should be based upon data that point to the success or failure of the dual-credit program.

Support open inquiry and honest responses. For all parties to fully trust the integrity of the administration and the planning team, they must feel that they can inquire about issues without fear of retaliation, as mentioned earlier in this inclusion model. The administration and the planning team must repeatedly demonstrate prompt, aboveboard follow-through on its commitments.

Widespread, systemic involvement in educational changes helps avoid some of the issues that could become impediments to an effective process. Administrators should not be reluctant to make decisions independently; however, sound wisdom indicates that it is important to have the input of those who will implement the initiatives. Thus the administration should build a broad base of support via the planning team to develop and implement a workable plan. As a collateral benefit, the planning team claims ownership in the process and helps build support among others within the institution.

Reference Glossary

Systemic change. Pervasive change that affects every component of an organization or institution.

Inclusion methodology. A process that allows constituent groups to play an active role in the decision-making and change-effecting process.

8

Conclusion

A well-educated, well-trained citizenry is very important. Thus it is essential that school administrators exercise authority in reevaluating conventional educational practices. Those practices that will aid in developing a well-educated and well-trained citizenry for the 21st century should, of course, be maintained. But those practices that prepare students in competencies that are obsolete, for jobs that no longer exist, and in ways that are outmoded should be abandoned. Innovative educational practices should be adopted, when appropriate, to provide students with maximum opportunities for quality education. Dual credit is one such practice.

Schools can no longer afford to keep students on a "slow track," educationally. If students are cognitively prepared to take on greater educational challenges, every avenue should be made available to support them and to allow them educational access. In the 1880s, it was considered an "evil" when secondary and postsecondary schools did not partner. Today, it is an "evil" when capable students are denied an opportunity to accelerate their learning. Hopefully, this book helps eliminate the barriers to accelerated learning and helps topple the obstacles to implementing quality dual-credit programs. Further, it is hoped that the academic purists, those who once openly resisted change or, in some instances, remained silent yet immovable on the issue of dual-credit programs, will reevaluate their positions and help create paths for more students to gain the knowledge and skills necessary to advance their education, make contributions to society, and, hopefully, create a more socioeconomically secure future for us all.

Discussion Questions

1. What should be the role of the administrators (e.g., the high school's principal and the college's academic vice president) in creating dual-credit programs?

2. How should faculty be involved in developing the dual-credit initiative?

3. What are the differences between college prep and tech prep? Explain how dual credit and tech prep can promote a continuum of learning for students enrolled in both the academic and technical programs of study.

4. What are the philosophical positions (pros and cons) about dual credit? To which position do you subscribe, and why?

5. What is the efficacy of dual credit with respect to its ability to challenge students? If dual credit does not provide this end result, explain why.

6. What is articulation, and what are its pros and cons?

7. What are educational degree plans? Why should students be encouraged to develop a personalized degree plan by the time they complete 12 semester–credit hours?

8. What are the pros and cons of parental involvement in the educational programs of the secondary and postsecondary schools?

9. What are the differences between an educational objective and an educational competency? Provide examples of each.

10. How do discipline teams function in the dual-credit process?

11. Distance education affords students the opportunity to remain at their home site and receive college-level instruction and credit. What are some of the challenges associated with this mode of instructional delivery for dual-credit classes?

12. As you critique the Annotated Implementation Model, which parts of it do not apply to your institution? What additional components should be added?

13. Should dual-credit courses that are taught at the high school campus only employ high school teachers who are qualified to teach college courses? Explain.

14. How can accountability and effectiveness be demonstrated in the dual-credit program?

15. What is the difference between articulated credit and dual credit?

16. Should stakeholder groups be provided with qualitative and quantitative data about the dual-credit program? Explain the pros and cons.

17. Follow-up studies of dual-credit students are important. What follow-up methods do you propose, and why do you think such methods are effective?

18. What are the special mandates in local, state, licensing, and accrediting agency guidelines that restrict how you operate the instructional program? Explain.

19. What special strategies can be used to prepare high-risk groups of students to enroll in dual-credit programs?

20. Explain the concept of systemic change. What actions cause the systemic-change process to result in positive change? What actions cause the process to damage the organization?

References

Ford, M. L. (1979). The development of an instrument for assessing levels of ethnicity in public school teachers (Doctoral dissertation, University of Houston, 1979). *Dissertation Abstracts International, XL,* No. 3.

Ford, M. L. (1995, Fall). Dual credit should be institutionalized. *Alliance, 3*(2), 7. (Available from the National Center for Urban Partnerships)

Gaines, B. C., & Wilbur, F. P. (1985). Early instruction in the high school: Syracuse's Project Advance. In W. T. Daly (Ed.)., *College-school collaboration: Appraising the major approaches. New directions for teaching and learning* (No. 24, pp. 27-35). San Francisco: Jossey-Bass.

Gardner, D. P., et al. (1983). *A nation at risk: The imperative for educational reform* (Report of the National Commission on Excellence in Education). Washington, DC: U.S. Government Printing Office.

Hull, D., & Parnell, D. (1991). *Tech Prep Associate Degree: A win/win experience.* Waco, TX: Center for Occupational Research and Development.

Texas Education Code. (1995). Chapter 195, House Bill No. 1336. Subchapter A, Chapter 130 and 130.008. (*The Commissioners' ADA funding proposal for joint high school and college courses,* as mandated by the Legislature, was prepared and distributed to presidents and chancellors, Texas Public Community and Junior Colleges, by Commissioner of Higher Education, Dr. Kenneth H. Ashworth, "Concurrent Public School–Community College Enrollment Funding." October 13, 1995.)

Wilbur, F. P., & Chapman, D. W. (1978). *College courses in high school.* Reston, VA: National Association of Secondary Principals.

**CORWIN
PRESS**

The Corwin Press logo—a raven striding across an open book—represents the happy union of courage and learning. We are a professional-level publisher of books and journals for K–12 educators, and we are committed to creating and providing resources that embody these qualities. Corwin's motto is "Success for All Learners."